MUSICAL
INSTRUMENTS
OF THE WORLD

Stringed Instruments

M. J. Knight

W
FRANKLIN WATTS
Schools Library and Information Services

 An Appleseed Editions book

Paperback edition 2006

Franklin Watts
338 Euston Road
London NW1 3BH

Franklin Watts Australia
Hachette Children's Books
Level 17/207 Kent Street
Sydney NSW 2000

© Appleseed Editions, first published 2005

ISBN-10: 0 7496 6982 9
ISBN-13: 978 0 7496 6982 9

Dewey Classification: 787

Designed by Helen James
Created by Appleseed Editions Ltd, Well House,
Friars Hill, Guestling, East Sussex TN35 4ET

A CIP catalogue for this book is available from the British Library.

Photographs by Corbis (Art Underground, Cheque, Anna Clopet, GIANSANTI GIANNI/CORBIS SYGMA, MC PHERSON COLIN/CORBIS SYGMA, Pablo Corral V, Henry Diltz, Kevin Fleming, Michael Freeman, Rune Hellestad, Dave G. Houser, Robbie Jack, Kelly-Mooney Photography, Bob Krist, Barry Lewis, Chris Lisle, Gail Mooney, Gianni Dagli Orti, PACHA, Neal Preston, Bob Rowan; Progressive Image, Royalty-Free, Tom Stewart, Nik Wheeler, Adam Woolfitt, Conrad Zobel)

Printed in Thailand

Contents

Introducing stringed instruments

This book is about the musical instruments that belong to the string family.

Stringed instruments make a sound when their strings vibrate. The strings are bowed, plucked, or struck to make their sound. When they are played, the whole string vibrates from one end to the other.

The strings don't make much sound on their own. The vibrations they make pass to a thin soundboard underneath, which also vibrates. This makes the

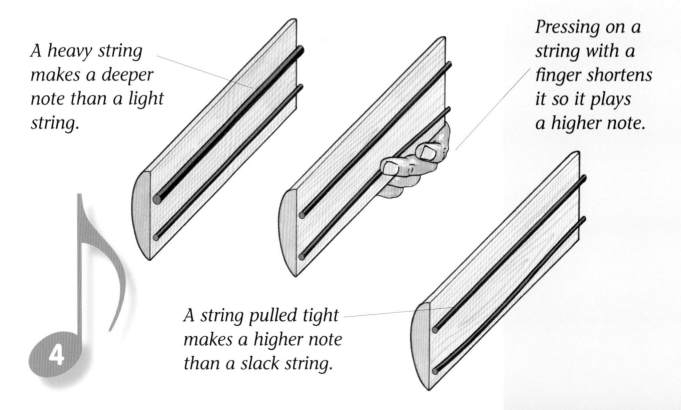

A heavy string makes a deeper note than a light string.

Pressing on a string with a finger shortens it so it plays a higher note.

A string pulled tight makes a higher note than a slack string.

4

sound louder. Some stringed instruments also have hollow bodies, which resonate to make the sound louder still. The sound holes in the body of the instrument allow the sound to escape.

The strings have to be strong and are usually made of nylon or steel. A light string makes a higher note than a heavy string that is the same length. String players can also make higher notes by pressing a finger on a string to shorten it. The tighter the string is, the higher the note it makes.

These violinists are part of an an orchestra in Venezuela, South America.

Violin

Violin Violin Violin

The beautiful curved shape of the violin was created in Italy about 500 years ago. The violin shares its shape with a whole family of stringed instruments: the viola, the cello and the double bass. As the baby of the family, the violin is small enough to be tucked under the chin.

The hollow wooden body of the violin has four strings stretched over it. When the violinist pulls a bow over the strings, they vibrate and make a note. The hollow body makes the sound louder.

Violinists put a soft pad under their violin to make it more comfortable to play.

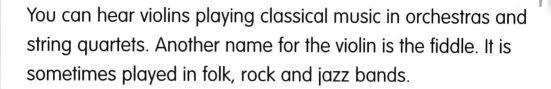

You can hear violins playing classical music in orchestras and string quartets. Another name for the violin is the fiddle. It is sometimes played in folk, rock and jazz bands.

Violins are made by hand from springy slices of pine or maple wood. The violin maker glues together two pieces of wood to make the front and two to make the back. A fine saw is used to cut out the curved shape.

The sides of a violin are called the ribs. They are made from strips of wood moulded into shape and glued between the back and front.

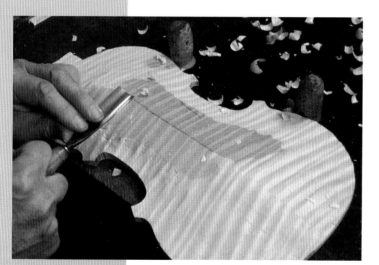

Two f-shaped sound holes are carefully cut out of the body. The carved neck and scroll are added.

ABOVE The violin-maker uses a sharp chisel to shape the back of the instrument.

BELOW Shaping the scroll of the violin.

Viola Viola Viola Viola

Big sister to the violin is the viola. It is still small enough to fit under the player's chin, but the sound it makes is lower and richer than the sound of the violin.

You play the viola's four strings with a bow in the same way as a violin. Viola players also make notes by plucking the strings with the fingers of their left hand. This is called playing pizzicato.

Most viola players belong to an orchestra (see page 11) or a string quartet. You do not often hear the viola played on its own as a solo instrument.

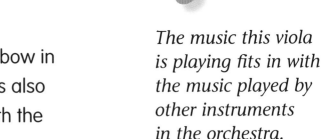

The music this viola is playing fits in with the music played by other instruments in the orchestra.

Cello Cello ♪ Cello Cello

Third in size in the violin family is the cello. Its other name is the violoncello. The four thick strings of the cello play lower notes than the strings of a viola.

To play the cello you have to sit down with the cello leaning towards you, so the scroll is over one shoulder. A metal spike keeps the cello off the floor. Cellists use a short wooden bow or pluck the strings with the fingers of their left hand.

Did you know?

Hairs from horses' tails are used to make bows for the string family. Smooth, pale hairs work best. You need 200 hairs to make a cello bow, 175 hairs for a viola bow and 150 for a violin bow.

The f-shaped sound holes let out the sounds from inside the cello.

9

Double bass

Double bass
Double bass

The double bass is the grand-daddy of the violin family. It can be more than 1.5 metres tall from the scroll at the top to the spike resting on the floor.

Double bass players stand up or sit on a high stool to play. When they pull a bow across the strings the double bass makes a low, round sound. You can pluck the strings too, to make a deep, echoing sound.

In jazz or folk music the double bass plays the rhythm. You will see several double bass players in an orchestra.

This is an American jazz band called the Brian Setzer Orchestra. The musicians are dancing as they play.

The violin family in an orchestra

The sound an orchestra makes comes from many different instruments. A symphony orchestra is divided into four sections: strings, woodwind, brass and percussion. It has about 90 musicians and plays classical music.

You usually find 30 violinists in an orchestra. The principal violinist leads everyone else. The strings are arranged at the front of an orchestra, and the musicians who play louder instruments stand or sit behind them.

A conductor uses his hands or a stick called a baton to show the musicians how fast and loud to play.

The string section of the Scottish Opera Orchestra rehearses in Edinburgh.

Harp Harp Harp

The first harp was inspired by the shape of a hunter's bow more than 5,000 years ago. Today, harps of many different shapes and sizes are played all over the world.

The orchestral harp is a big instrument, shaped like a triangle. It has 48 strings of different lengths stretched between the top and the side.

When a harpist sits down to play, she tilts the harp on to one shoulder. She plays the higher (shorter) strings

This Egyptian wall painting shows a harpist performing more than 3,000 years ago.

This harpist is playing at an open-air concert in San Francisco, California, USA.

with her right hand and the lower (longer) ones with her left.

Harpists can make a beautiful wave of sound called a glissando by brushing their fingers across the strings. The harp also has seven pedals at the base, which change the notes made by the strings when they are pressed.

Did you know?

The strings of orchestral harps are different colours to make it easier for the harpist to find the right one to play.

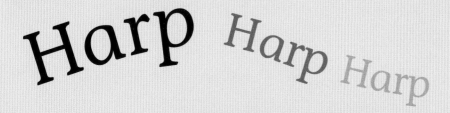
Harp Harp Harp

This lutenist is playing in a theatre production of a play by William Shakespeare.

Lutes are the oldest ancestors of the violin and guitar. People have played lutes for more than 4,000 years.

A lute is shaped like half a pear. Its wide neck ends in a pegbox, which is bent backwards at an angle to the neck.

Old lutes can have 20 strings. Covering the strings with four fingers is difficult and this is one reason lutes are not played often today. Another reason is that lutes are very hard to tune, and lutenists spend as much time tuning them as they do playing them.

Did you know?

The charango is a small lute from South America. It is made from the skin of the armadillo, a small digging animal that comes out at night.

Balalaika Balalaika

This Russian instrument grew up from the lute. Its wooden body is shaped like a triangle and has a flat back. People think of balalaikas as the national instrument of Russia.

You can play six different-sized balaikas. From the smallest to the largest they are: the piccolo, the primo, the secunda, the viola, the bass and the contrabass. This large balalaika plays very low notes. All balalaikas have just three strings.

Balalaikas play folk music, and accompany energetic Russian folk dances.

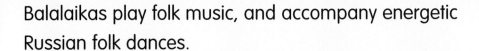

This balalaika is almost as big as its player, who is a member of a folk music group in Russia.

Mandolin

Mandolin Mandolin

The mandolin has a pear-shaped body, with a deep, rounded back. Many mandolins are beautifully decorated. They have four pairs of metal strings, which the mandolin-player plucks with a plastic plectrum to make a shimmering sound.

The mandolin comes from Italy, where mandolin players often play a tune (or melody) accompanied by a guitar. There are several larger-sized mandolins, which are called mandora, mandocello and mandobass. They are all played together in a mandolin band.

Did you know?

The mandolin is named after its shape. The word mandolino in Italian means little almond.

Steve Miller plays the mandolin in his blues band.

16

Bouzouki Bouzouki Bouzouki Bouzouki

This bouzouki player is performing on the Greek island of Rhodes.

The bouzouki is a Greek folk instrument. It looks like a long-necked lute and has a rounded, wooden body.

Metal frets divide up the long neck of the bouzouki, and it has eight metal strings. The strings are arranged in twos and each set plays the same note.

The bouzouki player plays a tune by strumming one set of strings with a plectrum.

17

Banjo Banjo Banjo

Hundreds of years ago the first banjos were made in West Africa from gourds (a fruit like a small pumpkin). The gourd was cut in half, and a piece of sheepskin was tied tightly over the top.

Today banjos have round, wooden bodies and steel strings: four long strings and a fifth shorter string. The banjo player picks out the tune with her thumb on the short string, and plays the accompaniment on the other four strings with her fingers.

The banjo is most often played in jazz bands.

Emily Robison plays banjo in the American country music band the Dixie Chicks.

Ukulele Ukulele Ukulele

The ukulele grew up from a Portuguese instrument shaped like a fish, called a machete. It is small guitar, which was first played in Hawaii. The name ukulele means jumping flea in Polynesian.

Ukulele players pluck or strum the four nylon strings, making a light, twanging sound. Ukuleles became very popular in North America and Britain during the 1930s. Today you most often hear them in folk bands.

These ukulele players in Kauai, Hawaii wear matching flowery dresses and flowers in their hair.

Did you know?

A cross between the banjo and ukulele was invented in 1925. It was called the banjulele.

19

The sitar is a famous Indian instrument. The body of the sitar was once made from a gourd (a fruit which looks like a pumpkin) and it has a very long neck.

Sitars have six or seven main strings, which are played with a plectrum. The highest-sounding string plays the tune. Up to 19 more strings are held by small pegs on the neck of the sitar. These make an echo sound when the main strings are played.

These schoolboys in India are learning to play the sitar.

20

Did you know?

Classical Indian music follows tunes and rhythms called ragas and talas. Different ragas are played at particular times of day, for example, a late-morning raga, or a night one. There are also special ragas for every season, which reflect the weather.

Every sitar has 20 metal frets across the neck, which can be moved to play different tunes. The sitar player changes a note by pulling a string sideways across a fret and making the note slide or shimmer.

Sitar players sit cross-legged on the floor to play. The sitar usually plays solos, accompanied by the tabla drums and the tambura, another long-necked string instrument.

Sitar players traditionally sit on the floor to play.

Zither Zither Zither

Hundreds of years ago African people stretched string between two posts in the ground to make a ground zither. They dug a hole under the string, and hit the string with a piece of wood to create a rhythmic sound.

Zithers are played all over the world. Europeans play board zithers. These shallow, wooden boxes have one straight and one curved side, with 45 strings stretched over the top.

Zither players sit with the instrument on their lap, or on a table in front of them. They play the tune with the right thumb. The fingers play the accompaniment on the other strings. The left hand holds down the strings to make the notes.

A traditional African ground zither – string stretched between two twigs over a hole in the ground.

Dulcimer

To play the dulcimer you hit the strings with small hammers. You can hear it played in the mountains of Austria and Switzerland.

These Finnish musicians are wearing traditional dress as they play their dulcimers.

Cimbalom

The Hungarian cimbalom stands on four wooden legs. Players tap the strings with thin, wooden beaters covered in soft cloth, which creates a warm, ringing sound.

This cimbalom is part of a gypsy band in Budapest, Hungary.

23

Koto Koto Koto Koto

The elegant Japanese koto has looked the same for many hundreds of years. Its curved wooden body is 2 metres long and holds 13 strings. Once the strings were made of silk, but today they are usually nylon.

Each string on a koto has its own bridge, shaped like an upside-down Y. The bridges hold the strings away from the body, so they sound more clearly.

Koto players wear plectrums like small thimbles, which fit over the thumb and first two fingers of their right hand. The koto is often played as a solo instrument, or to accompany other instruments or singers.

Did you know?

The koto plays the tune in a group of instruments which play gagaku – Japanese classical music. The other instruments are pipes called shawms, lutes and drums.

Yuriko Fujita kneels on the floor to play her koto in San Francisco.

The bandura is an unusual-looking instrument from the Ukraine, with a flat back and more than 40 strings. It is a cross between a zither and a lute, and sounds like a small harp.

A group of bandura players from the Ukraine.

Some banduras have two necks or scrolls. The low, longer strings run up the neck, while the high, shorter strings are attached to the body of the instrument. Bandura players pluck the low strings with their left hand, and play the tune on the high strings with their right.

25

The body of an acoustic guitar is shaped like a figure of eight. It comes from North Africa, and was brought to Europe 400 years ago. Today guitars play both popular and classical music all over the world.

Thin strips of metal called frets run across the fingerboard of an acoustic guitar. Its six strings are made from nylon or steel. The guitarist puts her fingers over the strings in different positions on the frets to make notes. Several notes played together create a chord.

This guitar player is plucking the strings with her right hand, while she holds them down with her left hand.

Guitarists pluck the strings with their fingers, or strum across them with a thin piece of plastic called a plectrum.

Dobro Dobro Dobro Dobro

This acoustic guitar has a metal resonator disc inside the body. The disc was added to make the guitar's sound louder.

Guitarists often play the dobro with a bottleneck, which is a metal tube fitted over a finger and pressed over the strings. Some rock and blues musicians play the dobro, and you can also hear it played in country music.

The metal resonator sits in the body of the dobro and makes the guitar's sound louder.

Electric guitar

The electric guitar plays rock and pop music. It has a solid wood or plastic body, and six steel strings. The fingerboard has thin bands of metal, or frets, across it, which show guitarists where to put their fingers.

Guitarists play with a plectrum. The vibrations made by the strings pass though a pick-up under the strings. They are made louder by a machine called an amplifier, which is connected to the guitar. The sound travels through the amplifier and out through speakers.

Did you know?

An man called Leo Fender invented the first guitar with a solid body in 1944. His most famous guitar is the Fender Stratocaster, which top guitarists still play.

You can see how this electric guitar is connected to the amplifier by a long lead.

28

Hawaiian guitar

The Hawaiian guitar (or pedal steel guitar) is an electric guitar which creates a swooping, sliding sound called a glissando. The guitarist moves a steel bar up and down the strings to make the sound.

Al Perkins plays country-rock music on his pedal-steel guitar in New Jersey.

Electric guitars in bands

Most rock and pop bands have two or three electric guitars. One is the lead guitar, which plays solos. The second is the rhythm guitar, which plays rhythmic chords. The third is the bass guitar, playing low notes beneath the other two guitars.

The bass guitar is made from solid wood or plastic, but usually has only four thick, heavy strings. It has a low sound and similar controls to six-stringed guitars.

Members of the band Dire Straits perform on stage at Wembley, in London.

29

Words to remember

accompany To play alongside a singer, or another musician who is playing the tune.

amplifier A machine which makes sounds louder electronically.

beaters Wooden or wire sticks used to tap or hit some instruments.

blues Sad and rhythmic folk songs which began among black slaves in the southern United States more than 100 years ago.

bridge A small piece of wood which holds the strings away from the body of an instrument. The bridge allows the strings to sound clearly.

classical music Serious music is sometimes called classical music to separate it from popular music. Classical music can also mean music which was written during the late 18th and early 19th centuries and followed certain rules.

country music Music which had its beginnings in North American cowboy songs. Also called country and western music.

fingerboard A strip of wood glued to the neck of a string instrument which players press to make different notes.

folk music Traditional songs and tunes which are so old that no one remembers who wrote them.

frets Small metal bars across the fingerboard of some string instruments, such as the lute or guitar. Frets help players find the correct position for their fingers when sounding notes or chords.

glissando A series of notes played fast to create a wave-like sound.

jazz A type of music played by a group of instruments in which each one plays its own tune. Jazz musicians often improvise, or make up, the tunes they play.

musicians Someone who plays instruments or sings.

orchestra A group of about 90 musicians playing classical music together.

plectrum A small piece of plastic used to pluck string instruments. It is also called a pick.

pluck To pull the strings quickly and then let them go again.

pop music Popular music which is entertaining and easy to listen to.

resonate To resound or echo.

rhythm The beat of the music, which depends on how short or long the notes are.

rock music Pop music with a strong beat, or rhythm.

scroll The carved top of a string instrument, such as a violin.

solo A piece of music played or sung by one performer.

string quartet A group of four musicians playing two violins, a viola, and a cello.

tune To adjust an instrument so that it makes the correct sounds.

vibrate To move up and down quickly, or quiver. A string vibrates when it is bowed, plucked, or hit.

Index